Between the words

Sue Lewis

Published by Cinnamon Press
www.cinnamonpress.com

The right of Sue Lewis to be identified as author of this work has been asserted by her in accordance with the Copyright, Designs and Patent Act, 1988. © 2025, Sue Lewis.

ISBN 978-1-78864-180-7

British Library Cataloguing in Publication Data. A CIP record for this book can be obtained from the British Library.

All rights reserved. No part of this publication may be reproduced, stored in a retrieval system, or transmitted in any form or by any means, electronic, mechanical, photocopying, recording or otherwise without the prior written permission of the publishers. This book may not be lent, hired out, resold or otherwise disposed of by way of trade in any form of binding or cover other than that in which it is published, without the prior consent of the publishers.

Designed and typeset in Bodoni by Cinnamon Press. Cover design by Adam Craig.

Cinnamon Press is represented by Inpress Ltd.

Acknowledgements

With much gratitude to Jan Fortune who set me out on my poetic journey and who continues to be such an inspiration.

Thanks also to my fellow poets in Sutton Writers, Mole Valley Poets and Poets Anonymous; to the haiku writers in Leaves to a Tree and to Rebecca Hubbard and her lovely Tuesday/Friday poets. Your support, guidance and friendship has been invaluable.

About the Author

Sue Lewis is a South London poet who began to write as a way of reclaiming her confidence after a minor stroke. Her poetry speaks with empathy and insight about how things are; the texture of our lives.

She has been published in poetry magazines, haiku journals and anthologies and was shortlisted for the Bridport Poetry Prize in 2022 and 2023. Her pamphlet *Written down in pencil* was published by The Hedgehog Poetry Press in 2024 and she has won the Cinnamon Press Pamphlet Award three times, previously with *Texture* in 2019 and *Journey* in 2021 and most recently with this pamphlet, *Between the Words*.

Contents

With us	9
Of autumn	10
Between the words	12
Third age	13
Drift	14
Filmic	16
Not quite	17
Thirst	18
Flame	19
Restless	20
Void	21
Tacit	22
Midsummer	23
Confessional	24
Altered	25
Things that are glimpsed	26
Hex	27
Of ravens	28
Hedge weather	29
Wilderness	30
Fossil	32

for all my dear ones

Between the words

With us

Morning spreads
across the painted floor

and sometimes, half-awake,
I'll meet a clarity so obvious:

a fragile, brief undarkening.

Then later, sitting quiet as lilies,
in a garden soft with shadows:

sudden swift epiphany.

Our need for pain
for poetry
for love

acceptance of what is.

Astonishing

to make sweet sense
of this rare music

understand we're not alone.
That we have never been.

An angel always comes.

Of autumn

No longer subject to
the pull of ocean tides

I do not navigate by
stars and moon

I float without a compass
on a calmer sea:

taste my own salt.

No longer ploughed
or harvested or grazed

I stretch out fallow-boned
beneath the tacit sky

watch ribs of trees
vault high above my head

and talk with birds.

I am a dry husk, paper-thin
bright seeds all blown away

a ghost who blind-walks
round familiar rooms

and haunts the backstreets
shortcuts, secret views:

forgets their names.

You were the mown path
through my thistle-field

your green grass sweet with
summer's felled remains

but autumn has a different taste:
celeriac and mud.

I watch for rain.

Between the words

We've shared the silence
of an unrequited life

our surface
swan-calm, glassy.

Underneath we're screaming—
tempted to the edge.

We stand well back,
choose from our jar of masks,
take refuge in the stillness—
in our safe space now.

This summer didn't go so well.
You're gravely ill.

The plans we made
we had to put on hold.

Already see how much
the days are shorter:
shadows alter, hour by hour.

We text:
you send me unicorns.

You're facing fire and poison
and we talk about

the weather.

Third age

We all become our parents soon enough:
my mother's ghost face sours the looking-glass.
Loose ashy hairs are trailing me around
my own tight rooms. My wardrobe's inked with black.

My hopeless lusts are tucked up, out of sight,
but still they threaten, crimson, at the hem.
I am so tired of turning up to death
with freshly-laundered words. Just let me be.

I want to read a newspaper unharmed;
drink tea, grow herbs beneath a quiet sky.
No flame can warm this freezing of my heart:
a winter of three layers stalks my path.

Drift

Sand is a brief page:

it speaks the language
of the wind and sea

and changes with the light.

I went to the beach

but the words I had left there,
the words I was searching for,
the words I was hoping to find,

had erased themselves.

Other words had come.

At the beach, early,
already there were footprints:

little sharp tracks of birds,
the damp tread of a man.

They will not stay long:
nothing ever stays.

Weather revolves around us:
water seeks to find its height.

A beach is a place
of conjunction;

of boundaries that shift.

But I remember.

Because I was
on this beach before.

Even now,

some of its salt
still clings.

Filmic

Above a winter lake,
entrancing corps de ballet of the gulls:
their perfect choreography.

Sharp silver kites.

Each movement perfect:
mesmerising in its
swerve and fall.

Duet of swans:
slow entrance
through the bowing ducks

their glistening heads
lit up by winter sun.

Soft shine:
a fraction brighter
each day now.

Not quite

Today I'm walking in the park:
green tips of daffodils
just spearing into gold.

Tight white snowdrops.
And the sun, for once,
half-grinning on the lake.

I walked here on the day she died:
same spring sunlight
but my eyes, salt-blind.

Then, three strange days behind her death,
that maddening stench
of roses. Not quite roses.

Something sweet and rotten
mixed within their musk.

Something awkward; transient.

Thirst

This granite afternoon
the rain is scattering down
like pearls, like wedding rice.
I taste of last night's
red wine sourness.
Empty. Dry.

I could write a letter to you,
pouring out my thirst.
But you are always
one poised step away,
measuring your stance.
And you know how to wait.

Now would be the time for music
but I can't think what to play:
you've taken all my notes.
Above my head the
green claws of the larch
reach lonely through the sky.

Flame

Mysterious moth
so pale and lovely:
how is it you are
drawn to me?

Curiously you circle
closer, closer.

So much I want to tell you.

Our open window
frames the evening
with a shape of longing.

How inviolate you are.

Night-flowers
scent the room:
the silence softens.

If I try to hold you
you will struggle, fly.
Damage both of us.

Your silver dust.

Restless

Through the silence
of the poem's space

my words
haunt this page

a hungry ghost
with much to say
of you & me

no peace tonight

the rain

still falling down like
willow leaves

like stars

or tears

I turn the line at its
enjambement, take
you with me
cannot   let you go.

Void

Hard to tell
where land meets sea:
all colours mute and veiled.

Cold clinging mist
salt-laden, sticky;
ghost-touch on my skin.

Damp fog-breath
glistens through my hair:
I turn my collar up.

The sea-birds silenced.
Not a sound.

My lashes wet.

As if with tears.

Tacit

We sit under white blossom
on the first really warm day
and something has shifted.

Something has broken free;
poured into this garden,
these trees and this sky.

I never thought of you as
someone who drinks tea:
there is so much
I do not know.

I know with certainty
the question mark
concealed within your smile;

the shape and colour
of your eyes.

They're storm-cloud blue.

White teacup in your hand;
soft linen tablecloth.

Late, fragrant afternoon;
small petals
decorate the grass.

This is so good, you say.
And I know you don't mean tea.

Midsummer

Sudden rain seed-pearls
the cat's black gloss.

I'm weighing my euphoria
against the awful cost of truth.

I'm so beyond, beyond
all possible redemption.

Yearning does not cover it:
what we
          did not say.

Somewhere, high up,
seabird voices. Wind-thrown.

Now these yellow roses.

Confessional

One hot and hollow day
let's take our skeletons to lunch—
I'll meet you by the Tube.

Blackening clouds, a sudden downpour:
intoxicating dark-earth scent
will rise from dust-dry pavements.

Sit with me. We'll share the wine.
Candles will bend forward to listen
though they've heard it all before.

Let's leave our shriven bones
inside that wine-dark cave.
Libate the final dregs.

Walk out to daylight and
a fresh breeze from the Thames.
Above us now, this clearing sky.

Altered

Later it may rain:
the air is heavy with its threat
and something in me
wants to see
this quiet canal stirred up
and altered. Fraught.

Here are wildflowers for you:
towpath buttercups and ox-eyes,
all alive and brimming with intent.
Your careful, cultivated life:
what would it take to wild you?

Things that are glimpsed

Ghost shadows
slipping through the dark

wind stirred ferns
that tremble at the moon

cat's cruel pounce
on velvet feet

the covert way
you check your phone
and smile.

Hex

My skin prepares to shed itself;
loose threads appear; unravel.

Solid thoughts become a clinging fog.
I wake now in the wolf-grey hours:
howl at my notebooks;
scratch down runes
that only I can understand.

The waxy pity of the moon
has nothing kind to say:
all certainties dissolving,
teetering on the brink.

I gather roots and bitter herbs;
wear midnight clothes; lean on a stick.
At dawn, sleek crows assemble,
murderous as a knife.
In the mirror I am turning into her.

I have a path to follow.

Of ravens

I have been so long at sea:
grey waves,
a charcoal sky.

Thick shrouds of mist
still block my way:
I search with sunstones
for the light divine.

My ragged sails
are pierced with holes:
now is the time
to send the ravens out.

Not finding land,
will you return,
dark messenger?

For I have grown
accustomed
to your shape;
your raucous speech;
the weight of you
upon my hand.

Your insight
of the day
that I must die.

Hedge weather

There was a time for saying things.

And if the words were left unsaid,
and if the paths were never taken,
maybe our green summertime
for saying things has passed.
It's autumn now and far too late.

Pick up the scattered leaves
and we might store them, brittle, dry.
Or we could make a bonfire of them,
watch them drift to aromatic smoke.

And set them free.

Wilderness

You say come.

And I—

cold rainswept stone
still winter-numb—

begin to think

if not now, when?

And so I go.

Your earth-bright palette
hawk-wing sky
wide spread of heat and light
and space

vast space

intrudes into
my cramped and frozen
monochrome

a splinter in the ice
just wide enough
to scramble through

exposing fault lines
I've pretended
are not there.

But now,
a thaw will come:
in time, perhaps,
a generous warmth.

Long overdue:
this risky, tender
pilgrimage.

Fossil

Late afternoon:
ripe pomegranate sun

the wild part of the beach
below the sea-kale and the thrift

rough rhythmic sea

rinsed pebbles

salty glare

it's there I stoop
to pick this stone

still in the shine
I sing and dance alone

neglected stone
which I will
warm between my hands

how you are there
inside of everything

the wild part of the beach

how things which seemed
long dead

can come to life.

www.ingramcontent.com/pod-product-compliance
Ingram Content Group UK Ltd.
Pitfield, Milton Keynes, MK11 3LW, UK
UKHW041342280325
456815UK00002B/93